HADDOCK

OR

HALIBUT?

Written by Alice Adamson
Illustrated by Alexander MacAdam

Haddock or Halibut? Copyright 2015
Written by Alice Adamson   Illustrated by Alexander MacAdam
ISBN: 978-0-9939022-0-8

Design and Layout: +MVM+
Louise Pierlot MacAdam

Published by   +MVM+
MacAdam Visual Media
8837 West St. Peters
R.R. # 2 Morell PEI Canada
C0A 1S0

With thanks to Mr. Adamson
and
Charlie, John, Joey and
Paul Adamson,
and

Albert and Florence Coffin
and
the other fisherman there
that day,
and
Alfred Laybolt
who started it all.

Copies may be purchased through
+MacAdam Visual Media+
Email: macadamvisualmedia@gmail.com
Phone: 902-961-2348

+MacAdam Visual Media+
www.macadamvisualmedia.com

Mrs. Adamson lived on an Island in the sea.

She lived with her family - her husband Mr. Adamson,

and their four boys, Charlie, John, Joey and Paul.

One lovely summer morning, Mrs. Adamson's neighbor Alfred dropped by. He was a fisherman, who had just come back from fishing, in his boat out on the water. He knew Mr. Adamson well. Mr. Adamson had often fished with his own uncle and his father, for lobster, cod, haddock, mackerel and herring.

Mrs. Adamson, didn't know all that much about fish and fishing. She had not grown up on this Island or grown up working at fishing, as had her husband. She was learning bit by bit about fish and fishing, even though she didn't go out on the water if she could help it. She knew she would always get terribly seasick.

4

Alfred very kindly gave her a piece of fresh haddock – no – sorry –
halibut, and well, to a fisherman, there is nothing better to eat than
freshly caught fish, straight out of the sea that same morning. She
thanked Alfred, and brought the fish inside to show to her husband.

Mr. Adamson was quite pleased to see this slice of fish, for that is what it was – or as he would say, a filet. He explained to Mrs. Adamson about haddock – no sorry - halibut.

"It's a flatfish - very large. When you catch it, you clean it."

Mrs. Adamson knew that meant to slit open
the belly of the fish, with a sharp pointed knife,
to clean out the guts - oops! No – innards.

Mr. Adamson said that the fleshy part of the fish would then
be cut off from along the backbone on both sides, top and bottom,
to make filets, using a very sharp knife with a specially curved blade.

"Then you take the filet and slice it across, like making a steak."

"You coat it with a little flour, some salt and pepper – not too much! and fry it gently in butter or oil...

...cook it first on one side...

...then turn it over to finish cooking on the other side...

...don't overcook it!"

But before cooking the fish, something else was needed....

Mr. Adamson liked to eat fish with potatoes, as was the custom of fishermen and their families who lived on the Island. This was because potatoes had always been grown on this Island, and there had always been lots of fish to eat as well. The best potatoes to eat were the dry kind, like perhaps Russets, or even blue potatoes.

At this time of year John could go out to the field
to dig for some early potatoes that were ready to be eaten.
Charlie and Joey went to pick yellow beans from the garden.
And the dogs came along to help, to look for field mice
or to chew on beans.

Mrs. Adamson had learned how to cook whole potatoes
with the skins on, until they were just done (not overcooked!).

After pouring off the hot water, and letting them steam for
a few minutes, she would peel them, holding them up on a fork,
slitting the skin with a small sharp knife and pulling off the peeling.
Ooh, ouch, that's hot on the fingers!

She would mash them and then leave them to
keep hot in the pot, until the fish was ready to eat...

...which should be almost right away!

Supper that day was a real treat – fresh haddock – er, no – halibut, and new potatoes, with butter, salt and pepper, along with fresh cooked yellow beans from the garden.

Are you starting to feel hungry?

"Mmmm!!! There is nothing like it!," thought Mrs. Adamson.
Unlike any fish that she had eaten, it was white in colour, and tender with
a delicate flavour, and a firm, almost meaty texture, a bit like chicken.

I don't know if her children enjoyed it quite so well, as they were not
overly fond of fish of any kind, although they did like lobster and mussels.

"That's okay," Mrs. Adamson thought. "I didn't care for fish when I was their age. Maybe they will grow to like it as they get older." She didn't tell them this however. Sometimes silence is a good thing. "Let them find out for themselves," was her way of thinking.

The Adamson boys knew they could count on having fish for supper on Fridays. Sometimes they had mackerel, sometimes smelts, sometimes sole, or cod, or halibut – er – no, sorry. I mean haddock. You see, fresh halibut is not always that easy to buy, but haddock – yes – I mean haddock this time, was more available.

Even so, Mrs. Adamson still got these two mixed up
and could never remember which name
went with which fish.

So she would ask her husband. He would tell her, and Paul, the youngest
of the boys, would fill her in on some of the things he had read about
haddock and halibut. Paul knew all kinds of interesting things about fish
and other creatures, and he always seemed able to remember many details
of what he had read. I think he preferred to see his fish in a book
rather than on his supper plate.

Mr. Adamson would explain that both
haddock and halibut are "bottom feeders".
They live on the ocean floor and eat whatever swims by.

A halibut – yes - she does mean halibut this time,
can grow to quite a large size. Mr. Adamson said his father
had once caught a halibut that weighed fifty kilograms,
or over one hundred pounds. A haddock – yes - haddock
is a much smaller fish.

Mrs. Adamson is beginning to remember which fish is which.

I mean, how can you NOT remember, after you hear that at first,

this fish looks like a normal fish, but THEN it CHANGES SHAPE!

It hatches from an egg and swims around and grows,

looking as most fish do, with an eye on each side of its head.

At six months of age one eye starts to MOVE AROUND TO THE OTHER SIDE of its head, and the fish begins to SWIM ON ITS SIDE, and BECOMES A FLATFISH with a broad dark brownish, greenish back, and white underside. Sometimes the eye will actually go THROUGH the head of the fish, to get to the other side. Mrs. Adamson thought these to be some seriously strange ideas to get used to thinking about!

Now the fish has two eyes, sort of side by side, but not quite, on the top side of its head. Inside the fish, the bones reshape themselves as well, and so do the internal organs. So this fish becomes flat but not quite flat. It looks like it's caught between trying to be a regular shape and a flat shape!

When it reaches this stage, it sinks to the bottom of the ocean and hides in the sand or mud, lying in wait for its food with only the eyes showing. It can raise and lower its eyes, and move them independently.

When a delicious morsel swims by, it leaps out of its hiding place and grabs it, with its large mouth, and good, strong teeth.

So if you live down there among the rocks and sand and mud it is best not to get too close to this fellow!

Halibut can grow to be REALLY big –
two meters long and over 300 kilograms
(six to seven feet and over 600 pounds).
That is as heavy as two BIG men together.

To swim around they undulate
their bodies in a sort of wave motion.
Can you undulate your arm?

Now imagine a huge undulating halibut!

After learning all about halibut, Mrs. Adamson shouldn't really have any more trouble to know which fish is which. This is especially so since she was in the grocery store where fresh fish was being sold, and she went to take a look at some haddock - yes – haddock. It looked like a regular, normal fish – NOT flat! It was darkish brown, as big around as will fit in your hands when you join your fingertips, and about the length of your arm.

It has a yellowish stripe running along each side from head to tail.

She noticed that the eyes were quite large and dark and sort of sunken, not rounded, almost as in pictures you would see of prehistoric fish.

Mrs. Adamson is hoping that one day she will be lucky
and see a real haddock – no – she means halibut.
Do you think she will then remember which
name goes with which fish?

I am not too sure about that.

But she knows a lot more about haddock and halibut now than she did

that day her neighbour brought her a piece of halibut - YES!! - HALIBUT!!!

Oh yes!

Before the end, I must tell you that this is a true story.

The people are real, though their names are disguised

and the Island is real too.

To see photos of real halibut
go to the
✛MacAdam Visual Media ✛
blog at
macadamvisualmedia.blogspot.com

The End